Tarot

Coloring Book

Major Arcana Cards

Aryla Publishing 2020

978-1-912675-87-6

www.arylapublishing.com

THE FOOL

THE MAGICIAN

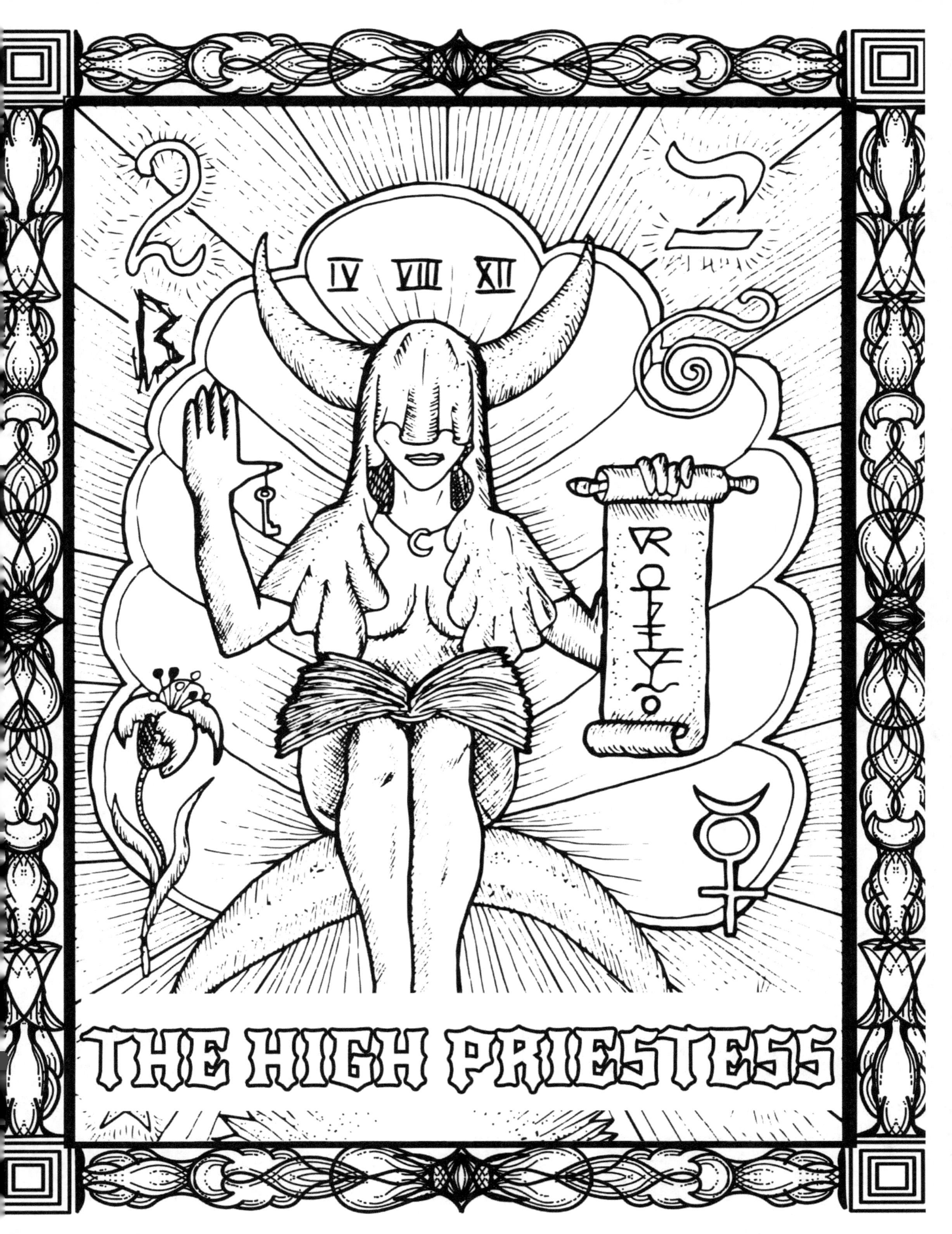
IV VIII XII
THE HIGH PRIESTESS

3
THE EMPRESS

4
THE EMPEROR

5
7
THE HIEROPHANT

6
THE LOVERS

7
THE CHARIOT

8
STRENGTH

9
XII
THE HERMIT

10
WHEEL OF FORTUNE

11
JUSTICE

12
THE HANGED MAN

13
DEATH

14
TEMPERANCE

15
DEVIL

16
THE TOWER

17
THE STAR

18
THE MOON

19
THE SUN

20
R.I.P.
200
JUDGEMENT

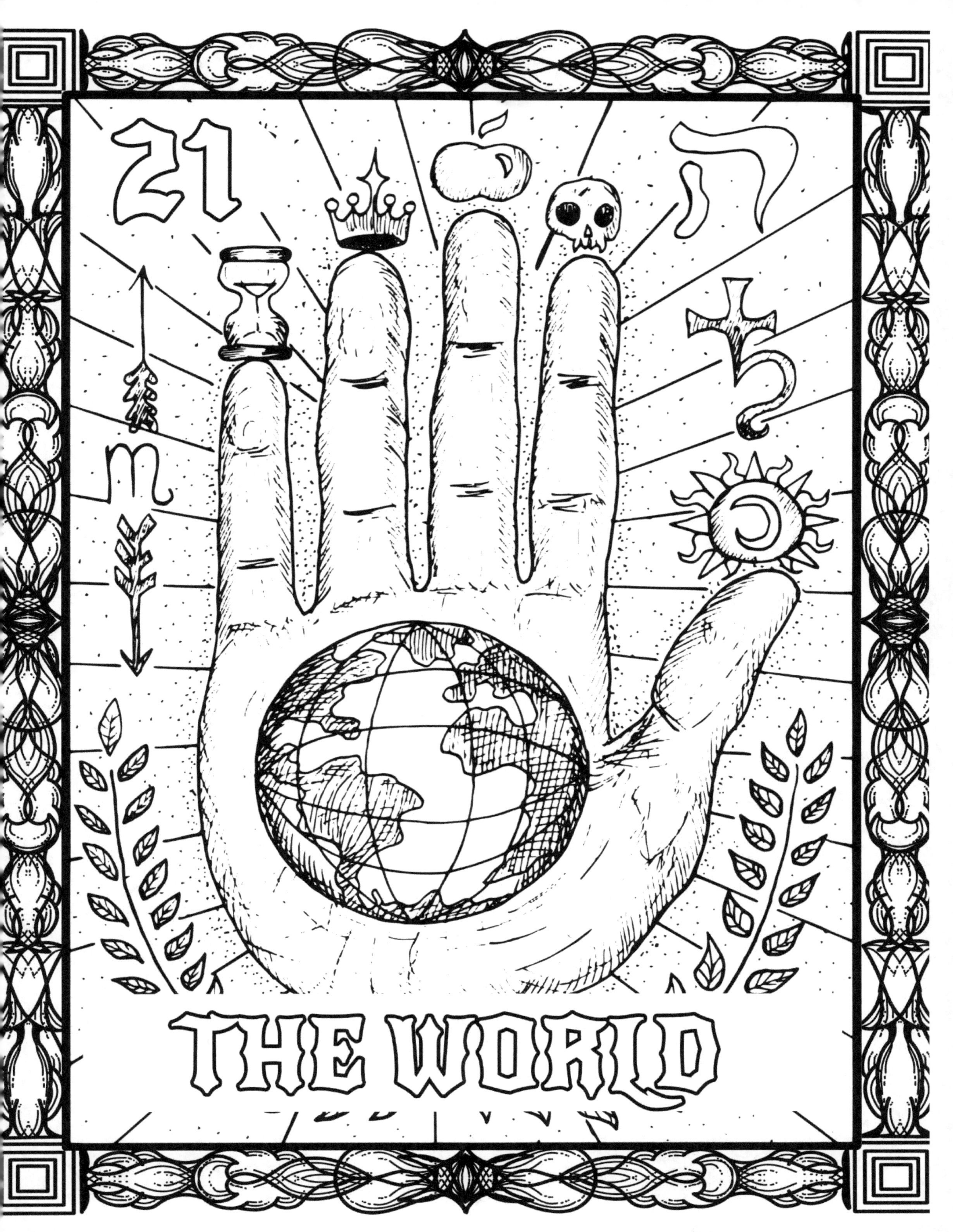
21
THE WORLD

Thank you for purchasing this book.

If you would like to know more about Aryla Publishing Books please visit:-

www.ArylaPublishing.com

Or follow us on
Facebook
Twitter
Instagram
for *free promotions*

@arylapublishing

We would love to know what you think of this book so please leave us a review.

Have a wonderful day 

Other Coloring Books from Aryla Publishing

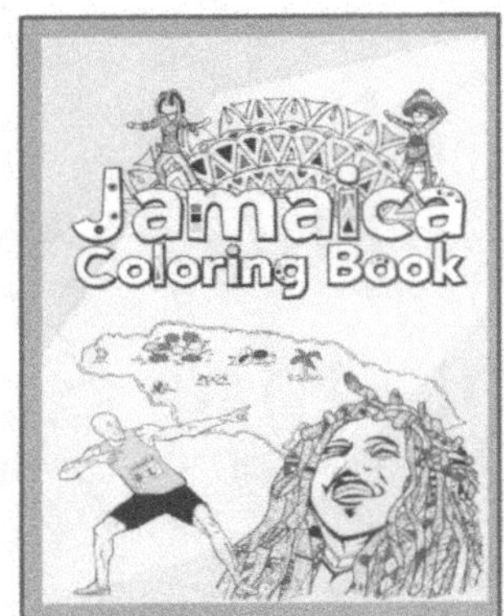

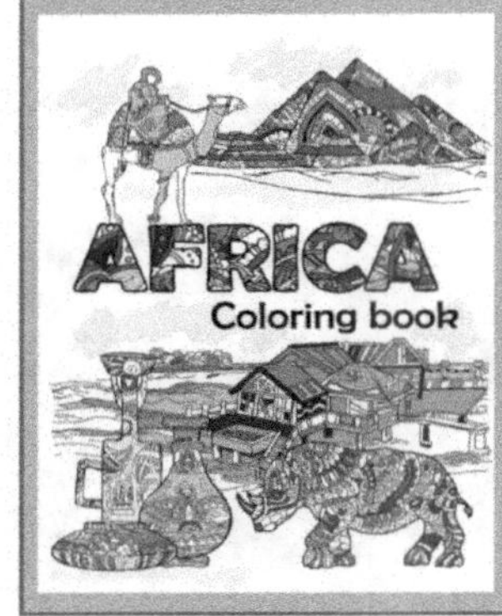

Merry
Christmas

UNDER THE SEA
COLORING BOOK

CHRISTMAS
COLORING BOOK

Spain
Coloring book

HALLOWEEN
COLORING
BOOK

MOTHERS
DAY

Fathers Day
Coloring
Book

HALLOWEEN
Coloring Book

SAME LOVE
Coloring Book

Valentine's day
COLORING
BOOK

BOOK

DEC
25
CHRISTMAS
COLORING
BOOK
North Pole

LOVE COLORING BOOK

HEALTH SERVICE
COLORING BOOK

Zodiac Signs
COLORING BOOK

SPRING TIME
COLORING BOOK

日本
JAPAN

GREEK
MYTHOLOGY

BLACK KINGS &
QUEENS
COLORING BOOK

BLACK HEROES
Coloring Book

MANDELA
& FLOWER COLORING BOOK

SCARY CLOWN
ADULT COLORING BOOK

CIRCUS
COLORING BOOK

ANIMAL COLORING
BOOK

MYTHICAL
CREATURES
Coloring Book

Butterfly
Coloring Book
Aryla Publishing

Color In Fun
Kids Books

Visit **www.ArylaPublishing.com**
to find out about all new releases.

Follow us @arylapublishing on Twitter Instagram & Facebook

Search for Aryla Publishing on

Check out our Book Trailers

Subscribe to keep up to date with new releases!

WE WOULD LOVE YOUR FEEDBACK

PLEASE LEAVE REVIEW AT:-